Essential AdWords

The Quick And Dirty Guide
(Including Tricks Google WON'T Tell You)

Kyle Sulerud

AdLeg Inc.
Grand Forks, ND

Essential AdWords
essentialadwords.com
adleg.com
support@adleg.com

ISBN: 978-1530701735

Table of Contents

About this Book

Let me tell you what this book is not. It is not a comprehensive, drawn-out guide to setting up and running Google AdWords campaigns – there are already plenty of books available that serve that purpose.

This is not a book that will explain all the little bells and whistles you can find in AdWords.

What this book *is* is a concise, hard-hitting, no-fluff guide to the most impactful features and capabilities of AdWords. Everything else you can do in AdWords is secondary to what you're about to learn.

The only subject that's as important as the topics in this book, that I won't be discussing, is landing pages. Landing pages aren't my primary area of expertise. Because of their importance, I've included some landing page resources for you in the online supplement section to this book, which you can find at EssentialAdwords.com.

To see if AdWords is right for your business (it's definitely not a good investment for many) go to adleg.com/adwords-score. You'll get a Search Network Score and a Display Network Score that tell you whether AdWords is worth pursuing.

Again, this is not an all-inclusive guide to all the bells and whistles in the AdWords platform. It includes information for beginners, and also has advanced strategies even the most experienced advertisers don't use effectively (or don't know about).

In fact, regardless of your experience level, if you don't get value out of this book, I will personally refund you for it. Just send a copy of your receipt to support@adleg.com and tell me you want your money back. Seriously. That's how strongly I believe the contents of this book will help you.

For supplemental material (videos, links, etc.), and to sign up for my mailing list, visit EssentialAdwords.com.

One last note: I have not held anything back while writing this book. These are my very best strategies and instructions. Because of this, you may feel overwhelmed or decide you don't have time to handle your AdWords campaigns effectively. If you would prefer to hand your account over to a professional, visit adleg.com/adwords-management to see how I may be able to help you. I've also included some information about hiring a campaign manager at the end of this book.

Now, let's get into the nuts and bolts...

Network Settings: Spend Your Budget Where It Matters Most (And The Little-Known Google Network That Can Make Or Break Your Campaigns)

When setting up your AdWords campaigns, you have the option to run your ads on different networks that Google owns. Here's a quick rundown of each one:

Display Network

Display network ads are seen all over the internet. Website owners sign up for a service called AdSense that allows them to display these ads on their sites. When someone clicks on one of these ads, three things happen:

1. The advertiser is charged for the click.
2. The website owner takes a cut.
3. Google takes a cut.

Display network ads can be image ads or text ads, and there are numerous sizes available. The most common sizes (if you can only create five banners, create these) are:

- 300 x 250
- 336 x 280
- 300 x 600
- 728 x 90
- 160 x 600

The display network includes millions of sites and is a very fast way to get your ads in front of thousands of potential customers. Display ads will also be seen on YouTube as pop-ups during videos. Because different websites have room for different types of ads, it is best to include multiple image ads and text ads in your campaign.

But here's the thing:

Most advertisers should not be advertising on the display network.
There are a couple main reasons for this. First, display network ads are usually seen while people are doing *other things*. This requires you to steal the user's attention and focus it on your product or service. Not the easiest thing to do.

Second, AdWords includes the display network in its default campaign settings. Because of this, there are thousands of advertisers with display network ads who have no idea they are even on the display network. More advertisers means higher costs per click across the network. While display network clicks are often cheaper than search network clicks, they are still higher than they should be based on how well the traffic tends to convert.

In spite of these issues, the display network can work well for some businesses. If you have a product or service that serves a specific demographic, and you are able to target this demographic in AdWords, then the display network is definitely worth testing.

Remarketing

Remarketing campaigns are the exception to the "you probably shouldn't advertise on the display network" rule.

You first create an audience by placing a snippet of tracking code on your website that will compile an anonymous list of your website visitors. You can also get this data by linking your AdWords account to your Google Analytics account.

Once your audience has been compiled, you can then create a remarketing campaign to show your ads to just these people. Because people who have already been to your website have a higher likelihood to buy, these ads become a much better investment than other display ads.

Some advanced remarketing strategies (you will need to link your Analytics account for some of these):

- Create time-based remarketing audiences based on the user's first visit on your site, or based on the most recent time they've been to your site. Create different ads and landing pages for each segment of users (i.e. 1-5 days, 6-10 days, etc.). This will keep your ads fresh over time, and allow you to advertise new features, benefits, and offers to people who have not yet made a purchase. Make sure you use audience exclusions in your ad groups so your audiences do not overlap.

- Create remarketing audiences based on which pages of your website were viewed. Build ads to remind your audience of this content and bring them back to make a purchase.

- Create remarketing audiences based on how long people spent on your site and/or how many times they have been to your site. People who visit your site often and stay on the site for longer than average are usually worth investing more in.

- Create remarketing audiences based on the keyword (paid or organic) that originally brought the user to your website. Do this with your most popular keywords in order to match the messaging of your ads to the customer's original search query.

- Create remarketing audiences based on the visitor's original traffic source. For example, if you've been getting a lot of traffic from a Facebook campaign, or from a guest blog post, then you can create specific remarketing ads that will target people who came from these sources.

If that doesn't get your idea-juices flowing, then I don't know what will.

Most companies should be running remarketing campaigns. If you're doing nothing else with AdWords you should at least have a remarketing campaign. Companies that shouldn't spend money on any type of display network ads, including remarketing ads, are "I need you now" services (taxis, locksmiths, emergency roof repair, etc.)

Advanced Display Network Ad Formats

The most common types of display network ads are image ads and text ads, which have already been mentioned. Some more advanced ads for you to experiment with are:

Lightbox Ads: These ads can include image galleries, videos, or a combination of both. This is one of the most powerful types of display ads. Yes, these are shown on the display network (not just on YouTube).

Animated Ads (general purpose ads): Google helps you create these by using your text and graphics. The elements can fade in, fly in, drop in, etc. The animation will help attract attention to your ads.

Dynamic Ads: Dynamic ads allow you to include different headlines, images, text, call-to-actions, and prices. Google then tries to match your ads to the content people are seeing, in order to create more relevant and compelling ads. Because these ads require you to give up a certain amount of control, they are not my favorite.

Search Network

The search network is what most people think of when they think of Google AdWords. You search for something in Google, and the top results are usually paid ads. These are text ads, so many people still confuse them with organic search results (even though they say "Ad" right next to them), which can be a good thing for us because people naturally assume the first link they see on Google is the most relevant.

There are some people who avoid ads and will only look at the organic search results. There are other people, like myself, who prefer clicking on

AdWords ads when looking for a product or service. In some respects, each traffic source targets different types of people. Search engine optimization (the process of getting a website towards the top of organic search results) can be a beneficial thing. But AdWords is just as important – if not more – because these ads are shown above any organic results.

Because Google is the place people go to find what they are looking for, search network ads are for companies that offer products and services people are already seeking. If you are trying to promote a new, unknown, or obscure product, then the search network probably isn't a good place for your ads to show.

Search Partner Network

As a supplement to the search network, Google allows you to show your ads on the search partner network. Google defines this network as:

A group of search-related websites and apps, including Google Search, Google Play and other Google sites, like Shopping and Maps. It also includes hundreds of search sites that partner with Google to show ads.

Basically, it's every website that uses some kind of Google search box, but that isn't actually Google.com. An example would be aol.com – do a search there and the results will include AdWords ads.

Another example is Google Maps. If you want your ads to be shown on Google Maps, you need to have the search partner network enabled.

The biggest problem with the search partner network, as of this writing, is that you can't be selective about it. It's all or nothing. So, if you want your ads to be shown on Google Maps, you have to allow them to be shown on all the other partner websites too. Another popular website for search partner ads is Amazon.com.

The search partner network can produce amazing results, or it can be a hidden financial strain on your campaigns. The performance data is usually much different than it is on the normal search network. Luckily, it's easy to find the data if you know where to look.

Here's where to look:

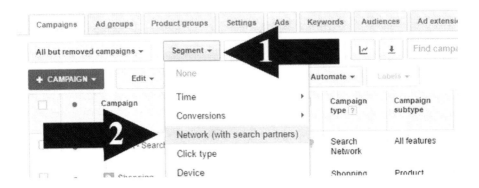

With the data segmented, you can see what your search partner performance looks like. You can do this from the "Campaigns" tab, the "Ad groups" tab, or the "Keywords" tab, and almost everywhere else where performance data is available in your account.

Here are a couple real examples:

Example #1: Good Performance

Ad group	Status	Default Max. CPC	Clicks	Impr.	CTR	Avg. CPC	Cost	Avg. Pos.	Converted clicks	Cost / converted click	Click conversion rate
			1,842	44,066	4.18%	$0.89	$1,648.52	1.5	166	$9.93	9.01%
Google search			1,652	29,167	5.66%	$0.92	$1,522.90	1.6	145	$10.50	8.78%
Search partners			190	14,899	1.28%	$0.66	$125.62	1.4	21	$5.98	11.05%

Example #2: Poor Performance

	Ad group	Status	Default Max. CPC	Clicks	Impr.	CTR	Avg. CPC	Cost	Avg. Pos.	Converted clicks	Cost / converted click	Click conversion rate
				2,943	94,363	3.12%	$0.29	$840.51	1.2	50	$16.81	1.70%
	Google search			2,406	40,651	5.92%	$0.30	$728.12	1.2	48	$15.17	2.00%
	Search partners			537	53,712	1.00%	$0.21	$112.39	1.2	2	$56.20	0.37%

For each of these examples, look at the "Cost / converted click" column. Notice the differences in the "Google search" row compared to the "Search partners" row.

You can see how important it is to know how your ads are performing on the search partner network. If they are performing poorly, you can go to your campaign settings and turn this network off. However, you may not want to turn it off completely.

Getting the most out of the search partner network

If you are getting SOME conversions from the search partner network (which is usually the case), then there are some strategies you can implement to focus on these conversions rather than turn the network off completely.

Strategy #1: Get rid of search partner network only queries

Go to the "Search terms" section of your "Keywords" tab. Just like I showed earlier, you can click the "Segment" button and select "Network (with search partners)" in the dropdown menu.

You will see a number of search terms that *only* have search partner data (or very little google search data). These search terms often have high impressions and low CTR. See the example on the next page.

Search term	Match type ?	Added / Excluded ?	Ad group	Clicks ?	Impr. ? ↓	CTR ?
Total				1,051	113,034	0.93%
cutco model 2018 homemaker 8 set includes 8 1759 table knives 10 kitchen knives & forks 1748 honey oak knife block 82 sharpener	Broad match	None	Knife Set	24	6,148	0.39%
Google search ?				1	1	100.00%
Search partners ?				23	6,147	0.37%
cutco 7 5 8 petite chef knife	Broad match	None	Chef Knife	3	815	0.37%
Google search ?				0	2	0.00%
Search partners ?				3	813	0.37%
cutco model 1759 table knife with double d dd serrated edge in sealed plastic bag with 3.4 high carbon stainless blade and 5 cla	Broad match	None	Table Knife	1	442	0.23%
Search partners ?				1	442	0.23%

What is going on here?

Well, there weren't six thousand people who performed a Google search for "cutco model 2018 homemaker 8 set includes 8 1759 table knives 10 kitchen knives & forks 1748 honey oak knife block 82 sharpener." This keyword phrase is basically hard-coded into a website somewhere, and is tricking Google's system. When anyone visits that webpage, this search term gets triggered and it displays an AdWords ad.
This usually isn't the kind of traffic we're looking for.

If you have search queries with high impressions from the search partner network, and virtually no impressions from the Google search network, then it's safe to say this isn't a search term people are actually typing into a search engine somewhere.

To get rid of this traffic, all you need to do is add those search terms as exact match negative keywords. There's a lot more on negative keywords later in this book, but essentially you would add a negative keyword that looks like this:

[cutco model 2018 homemaker 8 set includes 8 1759 table knives 10 kitchen knives & forks 1748 honey oak knife block 82 sharpener]

This usually works just fine, but in this case, that negative keyword is too long for Google to allow. So instead, we can trim it down and add a negative keyword that looks like this:

cutco model 2018 homemaker 8 set includes 8 1759 table

Do this for all your search-partner-network-only queries and you may start to see better overall performance from the search partner network.

Strategy #2: Create a "top-performer" campaign

If you've removed all of these keywords from your campaign, and the search partner network still isn't performing at a profitable level, there's another step you can take to capitalize on this network without wasting your budget on it.

What you can do is create a separate campaign for only your top-performing keywords. Leave the search partner network enabled in this campaign, and disable it in your other campaign. You can look at the Search Terms list to figure out which keywords are doing well on the partner network. Remove these keywords from your original campaign, and put them in your top-performer campaign.

Watch the results to make sure your top-performer campaign continues to do well on the search partner network, and keep adjusting as needed.

Strategy #3: Create a "search partner only" campaign

You can also set up a search partner network campaign (kind of). This strategy usually only works with nationwide campaigns in high-volume industries.

Take all those exact match negative keywords you found using Strategy #1, and add them as exact match keywords to a new campaign. You can't actually set up a campaign that only targets the search partner network. But if you've excluded these keywords from your other campaigns, and you add them to this new campaign, then you've essentially set up a "search partner only" campaign.

You can then run this campaign and optimize it like you would any other campaign, with the understanding that it will be a very high-impression and low CTR campaign. In order for this campaign to be profitable, you will likely need to set your bids lower than you have them in your other campaigns.

Because of how and where these ads are shown (as I showed you earlier), this campaign will behave more like a display campaign than a search campaign. Use caution.

Keywords: Get To Know Your Customers Better Than They Know Themselves

An AdWords campaign is only as good as its keywords. Some keywords are obvious. Others require some serious experience and testing to figure out if they're going to be profitable for your business. Others are just plain bad.

Keyword Selection

When setting up a campaign, people often try to cast as wide of a net as possible – including keywords for anything and everything related to their product or service. Google even makes this very easy to do with the keywords they suggest while you're setting up your campaign.

Here are just some of the keyword suggestions I received from Google while setting up a campaign for a website design company that builds custom websites:

- Be specific: avoid one-word keywords. Choose phrases that customers would use to search for your products and services.
- By default, keywords are broad matched to searches to help you capture a wider range of relevant traffic. Use match types to control this.
- Learn more about choosing effective keywords.

Enter one keyword per line.

Important note: We cannot guarantee that these keywords will improve your campaign performance. We reserve the right to disapprove any keywords you add.

An obviously good keyword on this list is *website design services*. Someone typing that into Google is very much in need of a website design company.

Some potentially profitable keywords would be *website design*, *website designers*, and *corporate website design*. People searching for these terms are possibly in need of a website design company. However, they may just be looking for general information, ideas, or even jobs. This is when conversion tracking becomes absolutely essential to a campaign (more on that later).

Some horribly bad keywords on this list include **design websites**, **how to design a website**, and **website design templates**. People typing these keywords into Google have a very low chance of converting. They are mostly looking for how-to information. They may click our ad (a costly click in this industry) out of curiosity, but they are definitely not looking to hire a company to build a custom website.

Remember, these are keywords Google is suggesting we add. With one click, we can "Add all from this category" and we'll have a huge list of keywords ready to go in our campaign. Unfortunately, the handful of good keywords are going to get crowded out by the abundance of bad ones. The campaign will most certainly be a failure.

It is essential to put yourself inside the mind of people typing various keywords into Google. Only select keywords that your target customer would be typing. The best place for you to find good keywords is your own head. When you run out of ideas, you'll want to use Google's Keyword Planner to make sure you're not missing anything.

Do a Google search for "keyword planner" and it will be the first result. Or you can go to my quick link **adleg.com/kp** and you will be redirected.

The Keyword Planner is fairly easy to understand and use. I've also prepared a video tutorial on how to use it, if you want some guidance. Find the video tutorial in the online supplement section of this book:

EssentialAdwords.com

Ok, so we've narrowed down our selection to a handful of keywords. Unfortunately, this isn't enough. We also need to be mindful of keyword match types.

Keyword Match Types

So let's say we want to be highly selective and just add one keyword to our campaign: *website design services*. We're ready to go, right?

Well, no. Not exactly. There are different keyword formats that will tell Google to show your ads for different types of searches.

Broad match

A keyword like *website design services*, in its raw form, is known as a broad match keyword. Here's what Google has to say about broad match keywords:

Broad match is the default match type that all your keywords are assigned. Ads may show on searches that include misspellings, synonyms, related searches, and other relevant variations.

Ok, so it's the default match type, and my ads may show on "related searches, and other relevant variations"? Is that a good thing?

In a perfect world this would make things easy. However, the keywords that Google's algorithms consider to be related and relevant are often very different than what we're looking for.

Here are just a few examples of keywords Google might show your ads for if you have *website design services* as a broad match keyword:

website design services
website design
web design
website design templates
website design school
website designer jobs
website building tools
websites

Clearly, we don't want to be paying for clicks from most of these keywords. We can use negative keywords to block many of these searches, which I'll discuss in more detail in the next chapter. However, there are more keyword matching options that will help focus more on the search queries we want.

Broad match modified

A broad match modified keyword might look like this: *+website design +services*

A plus sign in front of a word means that word must be included in the search query. Any words without a plus sign will be broadly matched. For this example, some keywords that might trigger our ad are:

website design services
website building services
website design services pricing
website development services

Search queries like *web design services* or *website design companies* would not trigger our ad in this instance, because they don't include both of our required words.

Alright. Now we're getting somewhere. Broad match modified keywords can be very effective, and I recommend including them in your campaigns as long as you have plus signs in front of your key terms (and a good negative keyword list).

Phrase match

Phrase match keywords look like this: *"website design services"*

The quotation marks tell Google that we only want our ads to show if this entire phrase is part of someone's search query. Some example searches would be:

website design services
website design services pricing
custom website design services
website design services new york city

Phrase match keywords can give us a lot of control over the types of search queries that trigger our ads. In some industries, we can even be profitable to use one-word phrase match keywords (again, you would need a good negative keyword list).

Exact match

This is what exact match keywords look like: [website design services]

Keywords in this format will only trigger your ads if those exact words are typed into Google, in that exact order. The only variations allowed are singular/plural forms of a word, and misspellings. So for this example, your ad would potentially show for:

website design services
website design service
website designe services

Exact match keywords are definitely the preferred type of keyword to use. But with so many people searching for things in so many different ways, it's impossible to know the exact match searches for all of them. Plus, Google only lets you target exact match keywords that are searched at least ten times per month, so you need phrase match keywords and broad match modified keywords in order to capture search queries that are less common or predictable.

You should also include exact match keywords at the heart of your campaign, but the other match types can and should be used as well. And using the other match types effectively requires a good negative keyword list...

Negative Keywords: Save Money You Didn't Even Know You Were Wasting

Negative keywords are critical part of an AdWords campaign. When I audit campaigns that other people have been running, the largest improvement to performance can usually come by adding more negative keywords.

Negative keywords tell Google not to trigger your ads when certain words or phrases are included in the search query. They're like virus protection for your AdWords account. In this chapter, I'm going to explain the basics of negative keywords, and then teach you some advanced strategies for finding them.

How do negative keywords work?

Let's continue with the website design example from the previous chapter. I think most people can understand the kind of traffic that would be good or bad for a website design company.

In the first list of broad match search queries I provided in the last chapter, these were some of the results:

website design templates
website design school
website designer jobs
website building tools
websites

We can easily exclude these searches, and other related searches, by adding these negative keywords:

templates
school
jobs
tools
[websites]

Notice the last negative keyword, [websites], is an exact match negative keyword. That means we are only telling Google to exclude people who are searching that exact term. For the other negative keywords on that list, we are telling Google to exclude any search that contains any of those words.

Since negative keywords require you to be much more specific than regular keywords, we would also want to consider adding the various singular and plural versions of each word:

template
schools
job
tool
[website]

If a word has common misspellings, you'll want to add that too. Google will not exclude a search query unless an exact word or phrase from that query is on your negative keyword list

How do I add negative keywords?

Negative keywords can be added in a few different places:

- Ad group level: This will exclude searches only in the specific ad groups.
- Campaign level: This will exclude searches for an entire campaign.
- Negative keyword list: This will exclude searches for every campaign the list is associated with.

Here's where to go in your account:

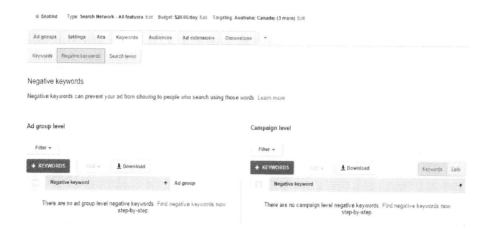

You can add keywords by clicking one of the red "+ KEYWORDS" buttons on this page, depending on whether you want the negative keywords to apply to a specific ad group, or to your entire campaign.

The main reason you might want to add negative keywords at the ad group level is to exclude keywords that you are targeting in other ad groups. Because of how Google matches your keywords to people's search queries, there may be search queries that can trigger your ads for multiple keywords. Adding ad group negative keywords gives you more control over which keywords are triggering which ads.

The place I recommend adding most of your negative keywords is in negative keyword lists. With a negative keyword list, you can apply your negative keywords to every campaign in your account, which is what you'll want to do for the vast majority of the negative keywords you find.

You can add negative keyword lists by clicking the "Shared Library" link on the left side of your AdWords dashboard, and then going to the "Campaign negative keywords" section. I also have a video tutorial on setting up negative keyword lists that you can find here:

EssentialAdwords.com

How do I find negative keywords?

There are numerous ways to find negative keywords. None of these methods will help you find every possible negative keyword you might need. In fact, I don't think a negative keyword list can ever be 100% comprehensive, because people will always search for things using a variety of words and phrases. However, these research strategies will help you block the vast majority of unwanted traffic from your campaigns.

Think of them yourself

Just like with regular keywords, some of the best negative keywords you'll find are ones you think of yourself. You know your industry better than anyone, and you should be able to think of terms related to your keywords that you don't want to pay for.

Use the Keyword Planner

You will also notice terms that should be added as negative keywords while you're researching your normal keywords in the Keyword Planner. In addition to finding keywords for your campaigns, you should be starting a list of negative keywords while you're using this tool.

Use Negative Keyword Pro

I built a tool specifically to help research even more negative keywords (it usually provides hundreds of possible suggestions). You can find the tool here:

negativekeywordpro.com

To use Negative Keyword Pro, you just enter one of your most general target keywords into the keyword box and click the "Get Suggestions" button. When I do this for *website design*, I get a results list that looks like this:

540 Results found!

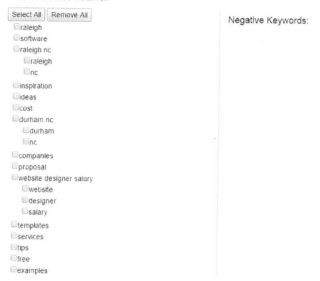

I can instantly see a number of words that should be added as negative keywords:

software
inspiration
ideas
proposal
salary
templates
tips
free
examples

The list goes on. All you need to do is check the boxes next to the words you want to exclude from your campaign, and they will appear in the next column over so you can copy and paste the into your AdWords account.

When you go to negativekeywordpro.com, you can watch a video tutorial that better explains how to use the website. My staff and I use this tool daily, and I hope you get value from it too.

View your search term report

Your search term report is located within the "Keywords" tab of your AdWords account. The search term report will show you all of the actual search queries that brought people to your ads. When you see search queries that don't belong, you can add them as negative keywords.

This is actually the most important thing you should be doing every time you log into your AdWords account. Excluding irrelevant search queries will save you money, increase your click-through-rates, and give you more control over your account.

AdWords has a helpful on-screen guide that walks you through how to add negative keywords using this tool. Just click "Find negative keywords now" and your tutorial will start.

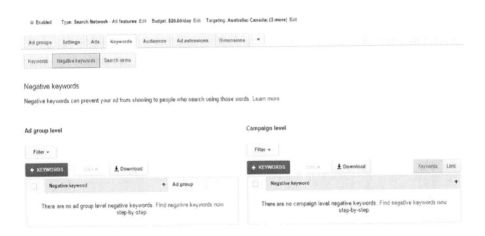

One thing to be aware of when adding negative keywords through the search term report is that the default negative keyword format is exact match. Usually, you'll want to remove the brackets so the negative keyword can exclude more than just that exact term. In many cases, it will also be best to add just one word to your negative keyword list that was part of the search query.

While you're adding negative keywords from the search term report, you'll be able to trim them down so they will be more impactful and will help exclude more irrelevant searches than if you simply leave them in their original exact match format. Remember to add singular and plural versions of the words you find as well.

Advanced strategies

There are some more advanced strategies I've developed that include the use of spreadsheets, and that take conversion data into account. These strategies are too technical for this book, but I've created video tutorials to demonstrate them. You can find these tutorials in the online supplement to this book:

EssentialAdwords.com

Conversion Optimization: Advanced Strategies for Maximum Profitability

When you're spending money on AdWords, it is essential that you set up conversion tracking. Without conversion tracking, it's impossible to know how well your campaign is actually doing. You may be getting a lot of clicks, but you need to track conversions in order to determine the value of those clicks.

AdWords is too competitive (and cost per click is too high) to ignore conversions.

With conversion tracking in place, you will be able to see a whole new level of data in your account. You will be able to see which search terms are generating your conversions, and the average cost of a conversion for each keyword.

With conversion tracking in place, you'll be able to see which of your ads are leading to conversions, and split test your ads for conversion cost instead of click through rate. It is very often the case that the ad with the highest click through rate actually has the highest cost per conversion.

Also, with conversion tracking in place, you can see when and where your conversions are coming from. Conversions will be recorded based on time of day, day of week, the user's geographic location, and the device the user was using (mobile vs. desktop vs. tablet). All of this data can be used to help optimize your campaign for better overall profitability.

There are different types of conversions and different ways you can track them. In this chapter, I'll be going over each type and when to use them.

I'll also discuss ways to optimize your campaign for conversions.

For technical instructions on how to set up conversion tracking, visit EssentialAdwords.com.

Types of Conversions

Form Conversions

To track the number of people who fill out a form on your website (contact form, download, free estimate, etc.), all you need to do is add a piece of tracking code to the "thank you" page for that form. If you have multiple forms on your website, you should set up different "thank you" pages for each form, and put a different tracking code on each one.

Sales Conversions

Sales conversions are tracked the same way as form conversions: Add a piece of code on the "thank you" or "order confirmation" page. With the help of a web developer, you can also set up conversion tracking to track the actual value of each sale. Obviously, some sales will be more profitable than others. Setting up your conversion tracking dynamically, based on values, will allow you to focus on revenue rather than just quantity of sales.

Email & Link Click Conversions

Yes, you can track emails using AdWords conversion tracking. What you do is set up your email address as a link on your website, and then track clicks on that link. You can do the same thing with other links on your website too – if the goal of your website is to get visitors to go to another website, then you should set up link conversion tracking.

Phone Call Conversions (From Your Ads)

This is a conversion that you set up in your AdWords account, and doesn't require any modifications to your website. All you do is tell Google to use a forwarding phone number in your ads. If someone calls the number in the ad (without even visiting your website) then the call will be reported as a conversion.

Phone Call Conversions (From Your Website)

This type of conversion is more advanced, relatively new, and the most overlooked type of conversion I see when looking at accounts. When website call conversions are set up, Google will dynamically replace the phone number on your website with one of their tracking numbers (a different number for every AdWords visitor to your site). Again, when someone calls the number they see, the call will be immediately forwarded to you, and it will be reported as a conversion.

Phone Call Conversions (Mobile Clicks on a Phone Number)

If you are tracking normal website call conversions (usually preferred), then mobile phone number clicks should not also be tracked. However, if you are not using website call conversion tracking, for whatever reason, then this is an option to track calls from mobile traffic. It is installed the same way as email and link click conversions. In this case, the click being tracked is the click on the phone number.

App Download Conversions

This type of conversion only applies to the handful of companies that use AdWords to promote their apps. You can set up AdWords to track downloads of your Android and iOS apps.

Third-Party and Offline Conversions

You can also track conversions that aren't necessarily made on your website. Basically, you need to capture the unique click ID ("GCLID") for everyone who fills out a contact/lead form on your website. Later, when that lead becomes a customer, you can import the information back into

AdWords and it will be tracked as a conversion. There are various third-party systems that use this function to help you track AdWords conversions.

Optimizing for Conversions

The reason for tracking all these conversions is so we can "optimize" the campaign based on the conversion data we acquire. I put that word in quotation marks because it gets thrown around a lot when people talk about their AdWords campaigns. The problem with the word, in my opinion, is that it implies perfection – that somehow the campaign will reach an "optimized" state where it is no longer able to be improved. This simply isn't true. There is always room for improvement.

Nonetheless, I will use the word anyway. Just keep in mind that I am talking about a process rather than an elusive end result.

Conversion optimization is probably the most important and difficult process to undertake in an AdWords account. Once everything else is in order, it's the primary thing that will determine the long-term success of a campaign. It's highly technical, and it's the main reason clients pay me thousands of dollars a month to manage their AdWords accounts.

I'll do my best to break down the basics of conversion optimization right now.

Essentially what we're looking to do is maximize traffic from the components of the account that are generating profit, and decrease or eliminate traffic from components that are not generating profit.

Depending on the kind of conversion tracking you have in place, and how much you know about your conversions (profit margin, value per lead, etc.), it can be very easy or extremely tricky to determine profitability.

Whether or not you know your exact numbers, you need to place a value on your conversions and use that value when optimizing your campaigns. This value will be our target cost per conversion. Sometimes it makes sense to start with a target conversion cost that is at or above break-even, as this will allow you to gather more data, more quickly, to eventually create a more profitable campaign. You can always adjust target conversion cost later.

When optimizing for conversions, we need to begin with the big picture and then start zooming in.

Campaign Conversions

If our target cost per conversion is $10, and we've already spent $500 on the campaign with only two conversions, then we've got a lot of work to do. In this instance, there's nothing we can really do to start optimizing for conversions. If the campaign is already set up according to the strategies outlined in this book, and the keywords in the search term report look good, a more realistic place to start would be with the website or the product itself. Maybe the website needs a serious overhaul. Or maybe the product just isn't right for AdWords.

Let's look at a better example. Here is a very early-stage campaign that has spent $678.32 and has generated 40 conversions.

Clicks ? ↓	Impr. ?	CTR ?	Avg. CPC ?	Cost ?	Avg. Pos. ?	Conversions ?	Cost / conv. ?	Conv. rate ?	Search Impr. share ?
148	3,370	4.39%	$4.58	$678.32	1.1	40.00	$16.96	27.03%	97.83%

Notice the high average position and high search impression share. If our target cost per conversion is $20, we're already doing great – there's not much room to increase our ad exposure. In order to get more conversions, we would need to loosen up our targeting a bit and add more keywords.

However, let's say our target cost per conversion is $12. Now we have some things to look at.

Device Conversions

The first thing I would look at is the "Device" section of the "Settings" tab. Here is what we see:

Device ↑	Bid adj. ?	Clicks ?	Impr. ?	CTR ?	Avg. CPC ?	Cost ?	Avg. Pos. ?	Conversions ?	Cost / conv. ?	Conv. rate ?
Computers		80	2,103	3.80%	$5.32	$425.83	1.1	25.00	$17.03	31.25%
Mobile devices with full browsers	--	51	906	5.63%	$3.34	$170.15	1.1	13.00	$13.09	25.49%
Tablets with full browsers		17	361	4.71%	$4.84	$82.34	1.1	2.00	$41.17	11.76%
Total		148	3,370	4.39%	$4.58	$678.32	1.1	40.00	$16.96	27.03%

With a target conversion cost of $12, we're not doing too poorly. It may be best to let the campaign run for a while longer so we can gather more conversion data more quickly. Think of it as an investment.

However, if we want to start optimizing, here is what we can do (there's a lot of math involved, but math is what's required):

1. Computers and tablets are combined when it comes to AdWords, so the data from these sources needs to be combined. This gives us 27 combined conversions from 97 combined clicks – a conversion rate of 27.835%.
2. Multiply that conversion rate by our target conversion cost of $12: *0.27835*12=3.34*. This tells us that to achieve a $12 cost per conversion, and if the conversion rate stays the same, our cost per click needs to be $3.34. Now we can go into the campaign and adjust our bids accordingly.
3. Now we look at mobile. Apply the same formula to mobile: *0.2549*12=3.06*. Since the mobile conversion rate is lower, we need to bid lower to achieve the same $12 cost per conversion.
4. To figure out how much lower we need to bid, take the difference in required bid amount and divide it by the required desktop/tablet bid amount: *(3.34-3.06)/3.34=0.0838*. So for our device performance to be more even, we would need to apply a mobile bid adjustment of -8% (applied within the second column of the screenshot on page above).

After we make these changes, things are definitely going to change. These conversions rates will not stay exactly the same, and there are other changes we'll make in the campaign that will affect overall performance.

In AdWords, however, inaction is a form of action. If you're not setting the bids at $3.34, you're setting them at a different amount. If you're not adjusting mobile bids by -8%, you're adjusting them by 0%. We're not proving a scientific theory here — we don't need to wait for statistically significant results before touching anything. We can change things now, based on the data currently available to us, and then continue to make adjustments as we go.

Ideally I would wait longer before lowering any bids. $12 may be our target cost per conversion, but if we're not losing money with the current bids (or if we're losing money that we can afford to lose) then it's best to keep things running for a while with the higher bids. Once we start to decrease bids, our traffic will slow down and the data needed to optimize the account will slow down with it.

But — if and when we want to start targeting a specific cost per conversion, *that* is how the math is done.

Let's look at some other adjustments we can make, assuming we need to start getting $12 conversions right away.

Location Conversions

The campaign we're looking at is targeting the United States and Canada. When we go to the "Location" section of the "settings" tab, this is what we see:

Location	Bid adj. ?	Clicks ? ↓	Impr. ?	CTR ?	Avg. CPC ?	Cost ?	Avg. Pos. ?	Conversions ?	Cost / conv. ?	Conv. rate ?
United States	--	129	2,959	4.36%	$4.74	$611.71	1.1	32.00	$19.12	24.81%
Canada	--	19	411	4.62%	$3.51	$66.61	1.1	8.00	$8.33	42.11%
Total - other locations ?		0	0	0.00%	$0.00	$0.00	0.0	--	--	--

The results are different enough for each country that I would actually set up a separate campaign for each (which is usually the case). For this example, however, we'll make our adjustments within this same campaign so I can show you some more of the math. We'll assume we've already set our bids at $3.34 based on our device performance:

1. To figure out our target CPC for the United States, we multiply the conversion rate by $12: *0.2481*12=2.977*. So we need to get from $3.34 to $2.97.
2. Like with the mobile example in the previous section, we need to find the difference and then divide: (3.34-2.97)/3.34=0.1108. This answer tells us to apply a bid adjustment of -11% to the United States.
3. Same steps for Canada: *0.4211*12=5.053*. $5.05 is our target CPC.
4. Since the target CPC is higher than our current bid, our math looks a little different: *(5.05-3.34)/3.34=0.5119*. In this instance, we would apply a bid adjustment to Canada of +51%.

Since we already have an average position of 1.1, it's unlikely we'll actually be paying that much in Canada (once your ads hit the top position your CPC pretty much stays where it's at until competitors start to drive it up), but that is how we can apply the adjustments.

I'll also note that since we applied a -8% adjustment to mobile, and since mobile has accounted for about a third of our traffic, we've actually applied an average adjustment of about -3% across the campaign. So if we want to really want to get specific we need to take that into account when applying the location bid adjustments. For the purpose of demonstrating the math, I didn't get that detailed.

Your locations may be split up differently. Your locations may be split up by city, county, state, etc. I'd be careful when making adjustments for specific cities and states, unless you have data from thousands of conversions. If you make too many adjustments, based on only a handful of conversions, things rarely work out as intended. Instead, I would mostly focus on any outliers – locations that are converting significantly better or worse than average – and only adjust those.

Ad Group Conversions

Our ad group data shows that each ad group is also performing differently.

Clicks [?] ↓	Impr. [?]	CTR [?]	Avg. CPC [?]	Cost [?]	Avg. Pos. [?]	Conversions [?]	Cost / conv. [?]	Conv. rate [?]	Search Impr. share [?]
85	2,005	4.24%	$4.71	$400.39	1.1	22.00	$18.20	25.88%	97.30%
44	1,039	4.23%	$4.12	$181.24	1.1	11.00	$16.48	25.00%	98.69%
13	169	7.69%	$5.44	$70.72	1.4	6.00	$11.79	46.15%	97.63%
6	157	3.82%	$4.33	$25.97	1.1	1.00	$25.97	16.67%	99.30%
148	3,370	4.39%	$4.58	$678.32	1.1	40.00	$16.96	27.03%	97.83%
148	3,370	4.39%	$4.58	$678.32	1.1	40.00	$16.96	27.03%	97.83%

We can apply the same kind of math to adjust our ad group bids. In this case, we would change the actual bid amount rather than applying a percentage bid adjustment.

1. Our top ad group has a conversion rate of 25.88%. Multiply that by $12: 0.2588*12=3.105.
2. Using that result, we would change the ad group bid to $3.11.

Repeat this for every ad group.

The exception would be the ad group with only one conversion. I would keep that one running for a while longer to see how it averages out. If we decrease the bid too much too soon we could be selling ourselves short. If the next two clicks produce a conversion (which is very possible) then we will suddenly have a much higher-converting ad group. There have only been six clicks in that ad group so far. Give it some more time.

Side Note:

You may have noticed by now that earlier, when we analyzed device performance, we already changed these bids. And now here we are, changing them again. What gives?

Well, that's somewhat of a paradox, and it's kind of the nature of AdWords. There are a lot of settings that can be changed that will affect other settings, and they often compound on each other. Let's say, for example, you've applied the following bid adjustments to a campaign:

Mobile +15%
Canada +15%
Tuesday +15%

You may have data that justifies each of these changes. But if someone on a mobile device, in Canada, on a Tuesday, searches for your ad, your bid adjustment for that person is actually +45%. Does your data justify that? Probably not.

So be mindful of those possibilities. If your campaign shows significant differences in performance among these options, consider splitting them up into separate campaigns. Perhaps you would end up with campaigns that look like this:

Canada + Mobile
Canada + Desktop/Tablet
USA + Mobile
USA + Desktop/Tablet

This isn't always necessary, but it can certainly be helpful if you need to avoid the compounding effects of too many bid adjustments.

Keyword Conversions

Once we have enough data, we can start to adjust bids for specific keywords the same way we were adjusting bids for entire ad groups. You keyword data will look something like this:

Clicks ?	Impr. ?	CTR ?	Avg. CPC ?	Cost ? ↓	Avg. Pos. ?	Conversions ?	Cost / conv. ?	Conv. rate ?	Search Impr. share ?
148	3,370	4.39%	$4.58	$678.32	1.1	40.00	$16.96	27.03%	97.83%
23	296	7.77%	$4.59	$105.63	1.1	7.00	$15.09	30.43%	100.00%
20	421	4.75%	$4.07	$81.47	1.1	3.00	$27.16	15.00%	98.77%
8	124	6.45%	$5.61	$44.87	1.2	2.00	$22.44	25.00%	100.00%
12	212	5.66%	$3.36	$40.34	1.0	6.00	$6.72	50.00%	100.00%

We're looking for keywords with high costs and low conversions. We're also looking for keywords with high conversions and low cost per conversion.

A high cost keyword with low conversions would be the second one down. We've spent $81.47 and received three conversions at a cost of $27.16 per conversion. This is pretty far off from our goal of $12 per conversion, and there has been enough activity that I would start to make some adjustments at this point.

Using the same formula we've been using – *0.15*12=1.8* – we find a new bid amount of $1.80. If we change the bid for that keyword to $1.80, then we will likely keep our conversion cost for that keyword under $12. However, it is still early in the campaign, and decreasing the bid that much will also cause us to sacrifice impression share and traffic volume. At this stage, I would decrease the bid by a smaller amount to give this keyword some more time to prove itself. At some point though, if we need to get our conversion cost down to $12, then we may need to sacrifice impression share and traffic volume in order to do so.

The bottom keyword in this example has a cost per conversion of $6.72. This would be a great keyword to increase the bid for, except we already have a search impression share of 100%, and an average position of 1.0. There is nothing we can do with the bids to get more out of this keyword. In this instance, the only way to get more out of this keyword is to come up with a new ad that will improve the click through rate and get more of this high-converting traffic to our website.

Search Term Conversions

We analyze the search term report the same way we analyze the keyword data. Any search terms that are getting conversions should be added to the campaign as exact match keywords. We can then bid on them using data from the search term report as our starting point.

Clicks ?	Impr. ?	CTR ?	Avg. CPC ?	Cost ? ↓	Avg. Pos. ?	Conversions ?	Cost / conv. ?	Conv. rate ?
148	3,370	4.39%	$4.58	$678.32	1.1	40.00	$16.96	27.03%
20	394	5.08%	$4.07	$81.47	1.1	3.00	$27.16	15.00%
11	96	11.46%	$4.81	$52.88	1.0	2.00	$26.44	18.18%
8	77	10.39%	$5.61	$44.87	1.0	2.00	$22.44	25.00%
12	192	6.25%	$3.36	$40.34	1.0	6.00	$6.72	50.00%
7	34	20.59%	$5.74	$40.17	1.9	2.00	$20.08	28.57%
5	8	62.50%	$4.86	$24.30	1.0	2.00	$12.15	40.00%
6	37	16.22%	$3.74	$22.46	1.1	3.00	$7.49	50.00%

In general, when you're looking through your search term report, you should be adding every search term you see as an exact match keyword (or a negative keyword). You need to decide whether or not you want to target every keyword. If it's a keyword you want, don't rely on a broad match or a phrase match keyword to capture it. Add it as an exact match keyword so you have more control over the bid.

Ads: Stand Up, Shout, & Get Noticed (By The Right People)

A well-crafted, engaging ad will bring customers to your website. For the most part, you want ads that accomplish this goal.

But there's a catch: A higher click through rate usually equates to a lower conversion rate.

Here is the data from two ads that were running in the same ad group during the same period of time:

Clicks ?	Impr. ?	CTR ?	Avg. CPC ?	Cost ?	Avg. Pos. ?	Conversions ?	Cost / conv. ?	Conv. rate ?
1,348	80,430	1.68%	$0.12	$165.15	2.7	67.00	$2.46	4.97%
715	74,167	0.96%	$0.12	$82.29	2.6	67.00	$1.23	9.37%

Notice the ad on top has a significantly higher CTR, and a significantly lower conversion rate. In fact, both ads generated the exact same number of conversions, but the ad on top cost us TWICE as much as the other ad.

I'll admit that this is an extreme example. But when you test enough ads you'll notice that this correlation almost always exists.

So what's going on here?

Both ads are attracting the same number of buyers to click on them, but the ad with the higher CTR is attracting a lot more non-buyers. This could be because the ad is written too well to trigger the user's curiosity, but your actual product or service is not of interest to them. There may also be a discontinuity between your ad and your landing page causing most people to leave and only the hardcore customers, who are desperately in need of what you're selling, stick around long enough to make a purchase.

When split-testing ads, you should almost always split test based on cost per conversion. The ad with the lowest cost per conversion will be the winner.

An exception to this would be if your cost per conversion is already so low that you can afford to pay more if it means you will generate more overall conversions. In this case, your cost per conversion may be higher, but your net profits will be higher as well.

Because of all this, it almost sounds like writing killer ads isn't that important, since you may actually pay the price if your ads are too good. However, getting customers to come to your website is still the number one goal of an AdWords ad. If people aren't converting once they get there, you need to look at the landing page experience, or the types of people and keywords you are targeting in your campaign.

With this in mind, I'll discuss what it takes to write killer ads.

The Headline

The headline is the part of your ad that will get noticed more than anything. You almost always want to include the target keyword in your headline. This can seem boring, but I've tested it so many times that it's really the only advice I can give. Creative and clever headlines simply do not perform as well as headlines that incorporate the target keyword.

If the keyword is short enough, you can add a word or two to spice things up. If the keyword is too long to fit in the headline, you *will* need to get creative and at least make sure it is on the first description line of the ad. There are two lines for the headline (Headline 1 and Headline 2) and they can each be up to 30 characters long.

It can sometimes work to put your company name in the headline. But the only time I've seen this work is if your brand name is highly recognizable (either nationally/worldwide, or in your local market). The vast majority of your target market needs to already be familiar with your company. If not, then you are wasting precious ad space by putting your name in the ad.

There are other exceptions too. If everyone else's ad has a keyword-focused headline, you can make yours stand out by doing something a bit different. If you do this, just be sure to test the keyword headline versus the non-keyword headline. Again, in my testing the keyword headline almost always wins.

Let's look at some actual ads. I'll refer to these examples throughout the rest of this chapter:

car insurance

All   Maps   News   Shopping   Images   More ▾   Search tools

About 93,000,000 results (0.78 seconds)

Progressive Car Insurance - Progressive.com
Ad www.progressive.com/ ▾
Compare Car Insurance Rates From Top Companies. What Can You Save?
Ratings: Selection 9.5/10 - Ease of purchase 9/10 - Website 8.5/10

State Farm® Official Site - Free Car Insurance Quotes
Ad www.statefarm.com/CarInsurance ▾
See Why Drivers Trust Us Most For Car Insurance. Get Your Free Quote Now!
Save up to 40% · Free online quotes · Local agents · 24/7 service
Ratings: Selection 10/10 - Ease of purchase 9.5/10 - Service 9/10
Insurance Questions? · Free Quick Auto Quote · Find An Agent

Affordable Car Insurance - Get a Free Quote Now
Ad www.metlife.com/ ▾   (844) 220-6448
Others Saved an Average of $507/Yr. Switch & Save with MetLife Auto & Home®
Insurance coverage: Special Parts, Rental Car, Total Loss, Car Repairs
Switch and Save · Free Quote · Online-Only Insurance · Find an Agent

General Insurance $18/Mo - General-Insurance.com
Ad www.general-insurance.com/Quote ▾   (866) 537-0281
The Cheapest General Car Insurance. (Get General Rates from $18/Month!)
Save 72% Now · Discounts Available · 100% Free Quotes · Lowest Rates Online

Here are the top ads I see when doing a search for *car insurance*. Notice three of the ads use the keyword in the headline. Three of them include their company name (which is okay in this case because these are all well-known brands).

General Insurance decided to include pricing in their title instead of the full keyword. Since they are positioned in the marketplace as a low-cost insurance provider, this is a good strategy for them.
Notice also that the Progressive and General Insurance ads have their websites in the headline. This is because these companies are not utilizing Headline 2. In mid 2016 the AdWords ad format changed from one headline to two headlines. This screenshot was taken a couple months after that change, and these companies haven't changed their ads yet. Someone should probably send them a copy of this book...

Special Characters

Special characters can be used throughout your ads. Since we see a couple being used in these headline examples, I'll address them right away. The two we see above are the registered trademark sign and the dollar sign:

®
$

These will draw extra attention to your ad – especially if you are the only advertiser using them. Some other special characters that I've seen in ads:

\#
%
@
( )
=
+
/
&
ε
™
©
?
!
i
-
—

—

*

:

" "

»

«

Visit EssentialAdwords.com if you want to copy & paste any of these characters.

Most any special character can be used in your ads **as long as it fits the context of your ads**. A human at Google will be reviewing your ad. If your ad uses special characters for no reason other than to draw attention to the ad, it will be disapproved.

Don't be afraid to try creative uses of special characters either. If your ad is disapproved, you can simply submit a new one.

Description Lines

Every AdWords ad has one description line. Sometimes the description text is split across two lines (usually on mobile). In the examples above, the descriptions all fit on one line. You have 80 characters to work with.

The description should include features and benefits of your product or service, and should usually include a call to action (a direction that tells the user what to do). Use the keywords in the description again if it makes sense. These are the description lines from our examples above:

- Compare Car Insurance Rates From Top Companies. What Can You Save?
- See Why Drivers Trust Us Most For Car Insurance. Get Your Free Quote Now!
- Others Saved an Average of $507/Yr. Switch & Save with MetLife Auto & Home®
- The Cheapest General Car Insurance. (Get General Rates from $18/Month!)

All of the ads include a call to action in the description, either at the beginning or the end:

- Compare Car Insurance Rates From Top Companies.
- Get Your Free Quote Now!
- Switch & Save with MetLife Auto & Home®
- Get General Rates from $18/Month!

These ads are telling the user what we want them to do right now. Notice the features and benefits are included within the call to action ("Free Car Quote" "6 Minutes" "fast, free quote in minutes").

URL Path

The Path (formerly called the display URL) is the website address that will be shown in your ad. The final URL (where someone will land when they click on your ad) can be as long as you want. The Path doesn't even have to be a working URL, but it does need to contain 30 characters or fewer, split into two 15 character sections.

Here are the Paths from our examples:

- www.progressive.com/
- www.statefarm.com/CarInsurance
- www.metlife.com/
- www.general-insurance.com/Quotes

If I type www.statefarm.com/CarInsurance into my web browser, I get a "page not found" error. Again, this doesn't matter for the URL Path, so you can write anything you want here, as long as the domain (statefarm.com) is the same as your actual link.

Progressive and MetLIfe didn't use their URL Paths for any extra words. This isn't necessarily a bad move. I've tested ads with and without extra URL Path content and sometimes the bare-bones URL performs better.

Call Extensions

Next to the display URL you will sometimes see a phone number (as seen in MetLife and General Insurance ads). This is a call extension and can be added in the "Ad extensions" tab of your AdWords dashboard.

You can set up call extensions to show your actual phone number, or to use a forwarding phone number. The forwarding number will be provided by Google. Each user will see a different forwarding phone number, so when the number is called, Google will know which user the call came from so it can be reported in AdWords as a conversion.

You can also schedule call extensions, in case you only want a phone number to appear in your ad during certain days and times.

Callout Extensions

Callout extensions are the most underutilized feature available in AdWords. These are basically short bullet point descriptions (up to 25 characters each) that will appear below your description lines, separated by small bullet points.

From our car insurance examples, here are the callout extensions:

- Save up to 40% · Free online quotes · Local agents · 24/7 service
- Save 72% Now · Discounts Available · 100% Free Quotes · Lowest Rates Online

Callouts are only showing for two out of the four ads. This doesn't necessarily mean the other advertisers haven't included callout extensions in their campaign. This is a part of the ad that is somewhat random. Sometimes Google will show your callouts, and sometimes they won't. The order of your callouts will also be randomly determined by Google's system and will always be different.

It should be obvious that you should be including callout extensions in your campaigns. They look just like your description lines, so you can basically double the overall length of your descriptions by including callouts.

Sitelink Extensions

At the very bottom of the ad are sitelink extensions. Sitelinks are clickable links to different pages of your website. The text of each link can be up to 25 characters. In our example, we only see sitelinks in the State Farm and MetLife ads.

State Farm® Official Site - Free Car Insurance Quotes
[Ad] www.statefarm.com/CarInsurance ▾
See Why Drivers Trust Us Most For Car Insurance. Get Your Free Quote Now!
Save up to 40% · Free online quotes · Local agents · 24/7 service
Ratings: Selection 10/10 - Ease of purchase 9.5/10 - Service 9/10
Insurance Questions? · Free Quick Auto Quote · Find An Agent

Affordable Car Insurance - Get a Free Quote Now
[Ad] www.metlife.com/ ▾ (844) 220-6448
Others Saved an Average of $507/Yr. Switch & Save with MetLife Auto & Home®
Insurance coverage: Special Parts, Rental Car, Total Loss, Car Repairs
Switch and Save · Free Quote · Online-Only Insurance · Find an Agent

The order of your sitelink extensions is, again, randomly determined by Google. They also might not be displayed at all.

You can also add descriptions to each sitelink. Sitelink descriptions are two lines, 35 characters each. If your descriptions are being displayed, then there will only be two sitelinks in the ad instead of four.

Sitelink extensions provide you with more opportunity to add appealing text to your ads. Don't simply label these the same as you label the pages of your website. Instead, include additional features, benefits, and calls to action.

Structured Snippet Extensions

Structured snippet extensions appear below callouts, and allow you to display a list of some type of product, service, or feature that you offer. There are specific types of lists you are allowed to add. At the time of this writing, these are the options:

Amenities
Brands
Courses

Degree programs
Destinations
Featured hotels
Insurance coverage
Models
Neighborhoods
Service catalog
Shows
Styles
Types

These options give us quite a lot of flexibility. The "service catalog" or "types" categories can apply to almost anything.

Just like with callouts and sitelinks, Google will not always display structured snippets, and the order will be random.

The MetLife ad is using a structured snippet extension:

- Insurance Coverage: Special Parts, Rental Car, Total Loss, Car Repairs

State Farm used the "services catalog" option to list their services. By including callouts, sitelinks, and structured snippets, they've been able to include a lot of information in their ad.

Seller Rating Extensions

Seller rating extensions can help add credibility to your ads. In our original set of ads on page 41, two ads included seller rating extensions:

- Ratings: Selection 9.5/10 - Ease of purchase 9/10 - Website 8.5/10
- Ratings: Selection 10/10 - Ease of purchase 9.5/10 - Service 9/10

Another type of seller rating extension includes stars, like we see in this ad from Esurance (found when searching *auto insurance*):

These ratings are coming from Google Consumer Surveys, or from trusted review partners. You cannot display star ratings from sites like yelp.com, or even from Google's own company review system.

Getting ratings like these to display in your ads is a very advanced process, and is only feasible for a handful of advertisers. I won't go into all the details here, but more information can be found at EssentialAdwords.com.

It's not part of the rating, but notice also that Esurance included "NorthDakota" in the URL Path. This wasn't part of my search query, but this is the state I was in when I performed the search. This would require them to have a separate campaign set up for every state, but I like what they did here. It shows me that the ad is more relevant to me here in North Dakota (even though it takes me to a generic landing page where I need to enter my zip code).

Review Extensions

If your company has received some good press, or a favorable mention on a reputable website, then you may be able to add review extensions to your ads. These extensions must be from a reputable third-party source (trade journals, news articles, etc.). You can't use individual reviews from customers or from user-generated review sites.

I'll provide some more information about review extension in the online book supplement:EssentialAdwords.com.

Location Extensions

If you add a location extension to your ad, users will potentially see the address of your store. They can click on it to get directions. Locations extensions are especially helpful for brick and mortar businesses like restaurants, auto repair shops, and dry cleaners.

In order to add location extensions to your ads, you must have a verified Google My Business account. Just link your Google My Business account to your AdWords account and you will be able to add location extensions for any addresses that have been confirmed.

App Extensions

If you are using AdWords to promote a mobile app, then an app extension is the way to do it. You can link your app download page (Android or iPhone) to your AdWords ad. When users click on that extension, they will be taken directly to the download page.

Price Extensions

As of this writing, price extensions are the newest type of extension. They're so new that I haven't had much time to test them, but they look like they'll be very beneficial for companies that offer products and services at set prices. You can list multiple items with a header, description, price, and link to a specific page. You can even include "From" and "Up to" ("From $10" "Up to $250" etc.).

Go to EssentialAdwords.com for more information on price extensions.

AdWords Campaign Managers

I'd be doing you a disservice if I didn't include a section on AdWords campaign managers. There are a lot of people and companies out there offering to manage your AdWords campaigns for a fee. In my experience, the bad managers far outweigh the good ones.

To quote copywriter Gary Halbert: "Nothing in business (or life) is more expensive than bad information."

This couldn't be more true when it comes to AdWords. You are paying Google every time someone clicks on your ad. I've seen too many accounts – even accounts managed by "professionals" – that were wasting as much as 50-90% of their budgets on irrelevant traffic.

Anyone can claim to be an AdWords campaign manager. AdWords offers a certification exam that can be passed in an hour without much real knowledge of what it takes to run a profitable campaign. After passing the exam you are officially "AdWords Certified." Don't let credentials like this fool you.

The absolute best way to find a good campaign manager is to get a referral from someone you know and trust. Try to get as much information as you can on the success of the AdWords campaign (maybe the person you know has no clue how well the account is actually performing). If things sound good and the campaign is profitable, find out who is managing it and see if they can help you too.

Short of a referral, there are some other things you can look for. The next closest thing is a testimonial. Look to see what other business owners have to say about the campaign manager you are considering working with. Ideally, you would find testimonials from people with businesses similar to yours. These people have put their own reputation on the line to vouch for work of someone else. Testimonials mean a lot.

Some of the best AdWords managers are ones who learned the craft by running campaigns for their own businesses – with their own money on the line. This is the holy grail. You can learn all the tricks and strategies available, but playing with your own money (and losing) gives you a much deeper understanding of how AdWords really works.

People who learned their lessons the hard way, and *then* learned all the tricks and strategies available, tend to be great campaign managers.

The most important thing to look for in a campaign manager are the results that are produced. No matter how good someone's testimonials are, or how highly recommended they come, you need to look at the results of their work. Performance results trump everything.

At a minimum, you should know how much profit your campaigns are generating for you compared to how much you are investing. Sure, one management company may be able to generate more profit for you than another. There's no perfect way to find the best one. If you're considering hiring someone who requires a contract, make sure there is an easy way out of the contract if your account is not performing well and generating profit.

To see if AdWords is right for your business, visit:

adleg.com/adwords-score

To learn more about my company's AdWords management services, visit:

adleg.com/adwords-management

To learn more about me, visit:

adleg.com/about